Thinking, Changing, Rearranging

IMPROVING SELF-ESTEEM
IN YOUNG PEOPLE

BY
JILL ANDERSON

Cover Design & Illustrations
by
Kathy Howell

TIMBERLINE PRESS,   BOX 4348,   ESTES PARK, CO   80517

THINKING, CHANGING, REARRANGING

Improving Self-Esteem in Young People

TIMBERLINE PRESS, BOX 4348, ESTES PARK, CO 80517

Printed in the United States of America.

This publication, originally entitled "Thinking, Changing, Rearranging: A Student Guide For Improving Self Esteem," was initially produced under a grant contract with B.E.S.T. Center, Eugene, Oregon, through a federally funded project. This printing represents the second revision.

ISBN 0-9608284-0-0

In the midst of winter,

I finally learned

That there was in me

An invincible summer.

—Albert Camus

TABLE OF CONTENTS

A NOTE . . .
TO PARENTS, TEACHERS, COUNSELORS

With both sadness and irritation I have observed huge monetary and energy committments to "academia" in our schools while the domain of emotional growth is generally left to the wind. We ply our skills at whittling away glaring academic deficiencies, but feel helpless in the face of the far more devastating erosion of self-esteem. The concern is there on our part, but the skills are not. This book is an effort to offer some direction in improving self-esteem of children ranging from upper elementary through high school age.

A first edition of THINKING, CHANGING, REARRANGING was written to accompany a class in Self-Esteem designed for hearing impaired junior and senior high students. Funding for a grant was provided by the U.S. Department of Education for administration at the local level through the B.E.S.T. Center in Eugene, Oregon. This revision is an expansion of that original effort.

Have you ever found yourself relating to a child who seems to have low self-esteem by trying to "fix" things for them? by contriving events so they would experience success, validation, love? by manipulating events so they wouldn't have to face pain? However well-meaning on our part, and however effective in gaining short-term results, these efforts probably reinforce the belief that both good days and bad are somehow tied to the power of external events. The child attributes the quality of his day to something outside himself; he remains blind to his role in creating his day, and thus is powerless to make changes in it. The belief is deeply entrenched in children that they "have to" feel a certain way, "because of" what happened.

But self-esteem must ultimately come from within each person, and so we best serve our children by providing them with knowledge and skills for taking control of their inner environment. As we guide them into the realization that they have power over the quality of their own day, it also means that we best serve them by letting go of the power that we once may have had over them. That can be a bit scary, because it can mean that they will no longer need us to feel good about themselves. Or it can be a relief.

The approach in THINKING, CHANGING, REARRANGING is a fairly confrontive one. The child is asked to take a good look at his own thinking, language and belief systems. He is given not strokes, but skills—tools for examining his own thoughts and beliefs to find the source for his own emotional pain, and then the tools for removing whatever blocks may be standing between him and a sense of higher self-esteem.

The approach here is based on certain premises. First, that events in and of themselves have little if any power over us emotionally. Second, that the power lies in the thoughts and belief we have **about** those events. Third, that emotions will tend to follow thoughts (postive thinking leading to emotional well-being, ''junk-thought'' leading to emotional pain). Fourth, that a change in thinking will bring a change in feelings.

I want to emphasize that this is a skill-approach. What the child learns is how to recognize thoughts that cause emotional pain, how to recognize beliefs that cause problems, and how to change thinking patterns to new language that is free of pain.

I wish to comment on one of the skills. It seems to me rather critical that one be able to distinguish a Fact from a Belief. This is not difficult, even for children, but it is a skill which has a great impact on how we feel. Look behind emotional pain and you will see a Belief parading around as if it were a Fact. Living as if Beliefs were Facts can be disillusioning—if not downright frustrating.

At the point where one acquires that skill, something very interesting happens. At the moment that we begin to suspect that what we had clung to as a "Fact" might simply be a "Belief" we suddenly realize that we don't have the whole truth but only a piece of it, and that there are OTHER PIECES as well. Seldom is this reached with joy. But it is ultimately a freeing experience, and the long term rewards will far outweigh the temporary discomfort.

The source of material for the book comes from a heavy reliance upon the theories found in R.E.T.—Rational Emotive Therapy. In particular, the written materials of Gerald Kranzler and the course content of Virginia Bzdek have both been extremely valuable and extensively drawn upon.

Two other people, both with fine, clear minds and tremendous insight, have influenced me in the course of many long conversations. Jon Garlinghouse and Lyndon Duke are making significant contributions to understanding the relationship between inner language and emotions through their work at Adversity Research in Eugene, Oregon.

USING THE BOOK

THINKING, CHANGING, REARRANGING is appropriate for use with children from the age of about 10 upward. For use in elementary schools, I would suggest an allotment of 3 sessions per week, 1/2 hour each, extended over a period of 10 weeks. At the junior and senior high level, the material is suitable for elective courses related to Human Potential or Psychology. It is equally helpful as a tool in counselling small groups or individual students. Groups, of course, have the advantage of possibilities for sharing, breaking down the sense of isolation and the feeling that "I'm the **only** one who feels this way." They also provide wonderful opportunities for role-playing.

Rooting out old patterns of negative thinking and irrational beliefs isn't easy. They're deeply imbedded, and often not very obvious, so it takes awhile for most children (and adults) to acknowledge that they even have any irrational beliefs, and then only gradually do they change them and begin to see the benefits emotionally. But that's to be expected because of the nature of habits, so we allow time for it all to settle in. On the other hand, parents have spent an afternoon reading the book with teenagers and have experienced immediate benefits to communication.

A workshop by the author, entitled IMPROVING SELF-ESTEEM IN CHILDREN, is available to train teachers, counsellors and parents in using the material and in designing an extended course. For more information, contact the publisher.

— Jill Anderson

1. Self Esteem

What is Self Esteem?

When we talk about how much we respect our-
selves, how much we love ourselves, how much we
care about ourselves, we are talking about "self
esteem." A person who loves and respects herself or
himself is said to have high self esteem. A person who
thinks he or she is not deserving of love has low self
esteem.

Most of us have self esteem that changes from time to time.
Sometimes it is high—we feel good about ourselves and who we
are. Then at other times we may feel really bad about who we are,
so we have low self esteem at those times. Those changes can
cause problems for us, especially if they happen quickly.

Where does self esteem come from?

Everywhere we go we see pictures and hear information that
affects how we feel about ourselves. We are surrounded by other
people's ideas of who we are and who they want us to be. Parents, teachers, friends, television, advertisements, magazines—all
tell us how we are and should be. And sometimes they all seem to
say different things. Our parents want us to dress one way, our
friends another way, television another way, and magazines still
another way. Who do we listen to? All the differences can leave us
feeling confused.

1

In discussing self-esteem it will be helpful to know a few things. Let's look at the chart below. Each area of our lives has an X after it. That X represents where we are right now. It may be that we are exactly where we want to be in that area. If so, we would place the second X (where-we-would-like-to-be) right on top of the X that shows where we are. If we are a long ways from where we would like to be the X might be on the other side of the dotted line.

	WHERE I AM:	WHERE I WOULD LIKE TO BE:
Family	X	....
Grades	X	....
Friends	X	....
Peers	X	....
Body	X	....
Personality	X	....
How Smart I Am	X	....

Where would you like to be in each area? And more important, how do you feel about that distance between where you are and where you would like to be? We can feel badly about that distance —hurt, frustrated, and angry. In that case, we can feel that we are not "good enough," and we will end up feeling low self esteem. Or we can accept the space between where we are and where we want to be and use it as a positive goal for learning and change.

It is also helpful to know how much other people influence how you feel about yourself. Below is a chart that will help you answer that question. Mark a spot along the line to show who controls your feelings.

When you get upset, who makes you feel better?

Me ●————●————●————●————● Someone else; Other people

When you are feeling O.K., who makes you feel worse?

Me ●————●————●————●————● Someone else; Other people

Who is in control of how you feel?

Me ●————●————●————●————● Someone else; Other people

Sometimes we realize that we give a lot of power to other people. We may depend on **other** people to make us feel good about ourselves. But what happens when they are sick, or are not around, or are too tired? If we can't have high esteem **without** them we are in trouble, so it is important for us to become the person who can make us feel good about ourselves.

This is a book about change. We are changing all the time, growing and learning all the time. If we have faith in ourselves we can change in ways that we want to change. We can learn skills that will help us to change our feelings.

ACTIVITIES

Role Playing to Expand Vocabulary of Feelings

Role play different situations where you felt one or more of these emotions. Share out loud, if you can remember, what your thoughts were while you were having the feeling. If you can't remember, share whatever it was you might have thought in that kind of situation.

VOCABULARY:	EMOTIONS/FEELINGS	
Angry	Terrified	Hopeful
Embarrassed	Worried	Hurt
Frightened	Loving	Impatient
Shy	Excitement	Insecure
Annoyed	Ashamed	Jealous
Depressed	Confident	Proud
Guilty	Desperate	Resentful
Anxious	Disappointed	Respectful
Nervous	Disgusted	Satisfied
Joyful	Frustrated	Stubborn
Cheerful	Grateful	Sympathetic
Despaired	Grouchy	Upset
Enraged	Confused	Worthless

2. Where Does Hurt Come From?

Feelings don't "just happen." They are not little black clouds that float around in the sky waiting to pounce on us. They happen for reasons; they always have a "because." We can understand our feelings, and we can learn about why we have them.

Feelings change. Sometimes they change very quickly. One minute we are walking down the hallway feeling happy and excited. The next minute we are sitting in the lunch room feeling rotten. Why??? If someone asks us "Hey, what's wrong? What happened?" we probably would have to say, "I don't know." The feelings changed, but we don't know why. Not understanding why feelings change can be frustrating. We can feel confused about what is happening, and we can feel out-of-control, like someone else or something else is in charge of our feelings. Sometimes it can seem as if we have no choice, as if we **have** to feel angry or sad or miserable.

This book is about those feelings. **We have two goals. One is to understand why we feel the way we do. The other is to learn how we can change our feelings to what we would like them to be.** Feeling bad is alright for awhile, but why would we choose to feel bad if we can learn how to feel good, or better, about ourselves?

What causes the pain?

Two kinds of pain are experienced by people: *Physical pain* and *emotional pain. In the physical world of things and objects, the source of pain is clear.*

5

PHYSICAL PAIN

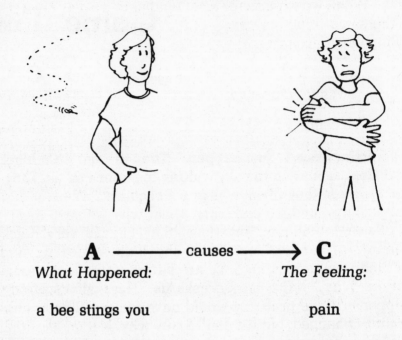

A ——— causes ——→ **C**

What Happened: The Feeling:

a bee stings you   pain

The person experiences physical pain **because of** the bee sting. In the example, **A** is the event, or what happened. **C** is the consequence, or what the person was feeling. **A** will almost always cause **C** in physical pain. Bees could sting five people and **all of those people would feel pain. They would not have a choice.**

PHYSICAL PAIN

A ——— causes ——→ **C**

What Happened: The Feeling:

BEE STING

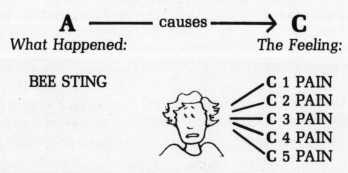

C 1 PAIN
C 2 PAIN
C 3 PAIN
C 4 PAIN
C 5 PAIN

What about emotional pain?

When we experience emotional pain we may have the idea that the same thing happens—that **A** causes **C**. We may **think** that it happens this way:

$$\text{A} \xrightarrow[\text{causes}]{\text{we think}} \text{C}$$

What Happened: *The Feelings:*

1. Joe called me "Shorty."   I felt angry.
2. Tim got a 'B'; I got a 'D'.   I felt frustrated, jealous.
3. Ann didn't invite me to her
   party.   I felt angry, jealous.

We think that we feel the way we do **because** we were called "shorty," or got a 'D', or, weren't invited to a party. We think that we don't have a choice in how we feel.

But in experiencing feelings and emotions, we do have a choice. Not everyone feels the same way when **A** happens. Two different people may have two different feelings. Five different people may have five different feelings! In a case like that we might see:

EMOTIONAL PAIN

A   **C**
What Happened: *The Feeling:*

Your teacher
didn't call
on you.

C1 Angry: ("That's the **only**
         answer I knew.")
C2 Jealous: ("Ted **always** gets
         to answer.")
C3 Happy: ("Thank **goodness!**
         I couldn't answer.")
C4 Depressed: ("She thinks I
         don't know **anything**.")
C5 Frustrated: ("She **never** calls
         on me.")

7

Obviously **A does not directly cause C.** If it did, then everyone would feel Angry or everyone would feel Happy, or another emotion.

What causes emotional pain? Not **A.**

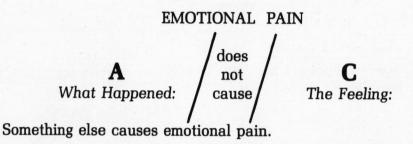

Something else causes emotional pain.

ACTIVITIES

Think of some situations in which the same things might happen to 4 or 5 people, but each person might feel differently about it. What are the different feelings and what might each person think?

A   **C**

C1 _____ : " _____ "

C2 _____ : " _____ "

C3 _____ : " _____ "

C4 _____ : " _____ "

C5 _____ : " _____ "

A   **C**

C1 _____ : " _____ "

C2 _____ : " _____ "

C3 _____ : " _____ "

C4 _____ : " _____ "

C5 _____ : " _____ "

3. Thoughts, Feelings and Thunderclouds

Emotions are not caused by events. Let's take as an example two people standing in the rain. As we saw in the last chapter, those two people can have two very different emotions about the rain. One person (C1) might feel happy, and the other (C2) depressed.

C₁
Happy

C₂
Depressed

The same rain fell on both people. Both people got wet. But look at their faces. They **feel** different emotions. Why?

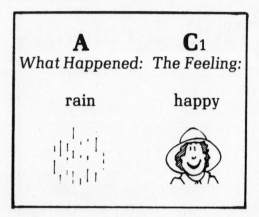

The only difference was what they each **thought** about the rain.

We will call those thoughts and beliefs **B**. **B** is what we think about **A**. So, it is not "what happens" that causes our emotions, but what we **think** about "what happens."

EMOTIONAL PAIN

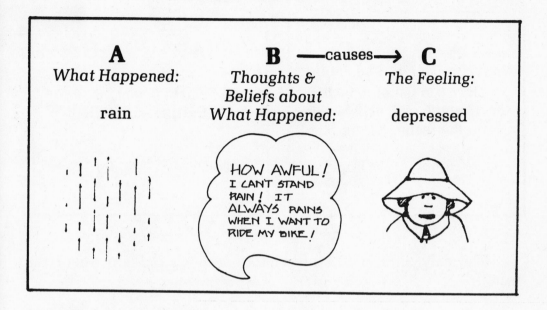

A
What Happened:

rain

B —causes→ C

*Thoughts &
Beliefs about
What Happened:*

The Feeling:

depressed

HOW AWFUL!
I CAN'T STAND
RAIN! IT
ALWAYS RAINS
WHEN I WANT TO
RIDE MY BIKE!

This person thinks rain is awful, so feels depressed. What would happen if this person changed their thoughts? Wouldn't their feelings change, too?

ACTIVITIES

Language is a Key to our Feelings

Here is a list of thoughts. Next to the thought is a blank. Read the thought and decide what you think the person is **feeling**. Write the feeling in the blank.

Happy   Depressed   Jealous   Angry

_____ 1. "Poor me! Nobody likes me."

_____ 2. "It's not my fault I lost it."

_____ 3. "I'll do better next time."

_____ 4. "That was nice of her to help."

_____ 5. "I'm fine just the way I am."

_____ 6. "Why should I bother; I can't do it."

_____ 7. "She always gets the best gift."

_____ 8. "I think getting a 'C' was O.K."

_____ 9. "You're just awful!"

_____ 10. "Everything is O.K. the way it is."

4. But, What About Vanilla?

We understand now that our bad feelings aren't caused by what happens, but by what we think about what happens. So, if we want to say good-bye to some of those bad feelings, then the first step is to start paying more attention to what we're thinking. We will look first at our Beliefs, then at our language and vocabulary. That's where we'll find clues as to why we feel the way we do.

There is a difference between a *Fact* and a *Belief*. A *Fact* is known to be true, can be proven, and is accepted by almost everyone.

Here are some *Facts:*

> 1. "Ice cream is a food."
> 2. "Bicycles do not create pollution."
> 3. "Math is a subject taught in school."

People would not generally argue with those facts, and it is hard to imagine anyone getting upset over them. Can you imagine someone being angry because grass is green? Of course not.

A *Belief* is an idea felt to be true by some people, but maybe not by others. A belief may be true at one time, but not at another. It is like an opinion. People might not say this part out loud, but a belief usually has "I think . . ." in front of it. Beliefs are often what people think about Facts.

Here are some *Beliefs:*

15

1. "Chocolate ice cream is great!"
2. "Bicycles are better for trans-portation than cars."
3. Long division is a waste of time."

These are beliefs that make sense. They may not be true all the time, or may not be true for everyone; but they can be true for some people some of the time. Because they make sense, we call them *Rational Beliefs*. People don't usually get upset over rational beliefs.

Here are some *Beliefs* that don't make sense:

1. "The best ice cream is **CHOCOLATE. Everyone** must like chocolate! All the other flavors are **awful!** Anybody who doesn't like Chocolate is **stupid!**"
2. "**Everybody** should ride a bike, all the time. People who drive cars are ruin-ing **everything!** They should be fined!"
3. "I flunked my math test 'cause my **Mom** made me runny eggs for break-fast! It made me so upset that I forgot all the long division facts! It's all **her** fault!"

These beliefs don't make sense. They are not true; they are ridiculous. We call them *Irrational Beliefs*. People who have irrational beliefs probably get upset a lot, just because of the way things are.

16

Which are Facts? Which are Beliefs?

Put a #1, #2, or #3 next to the statment.

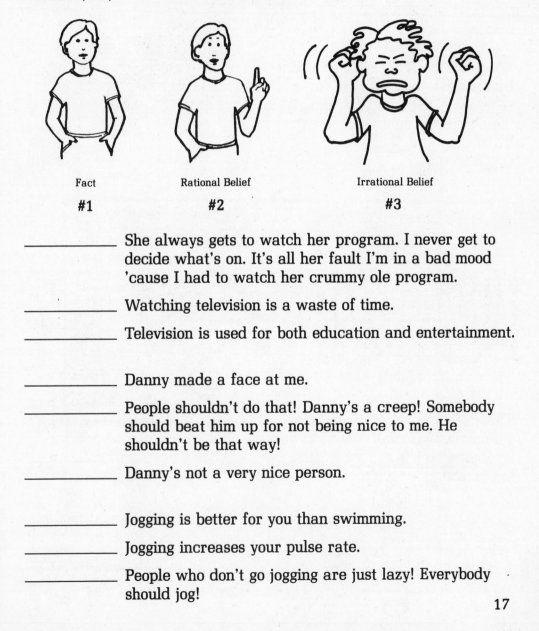

Fact	Rational Belief	Irrational Belief
#1	#2	#3

_____ She always gets to watch her program. I never get to decide what's on. It's all her fault I'm in a bad mood 'cause I had to watch her crummy ole program.

_____ Watching television is a waste of time.

_____ Television is used for both education and entertainment.

_____ Danny made a face at me.

_____ People shouldn't do that! Danny's a creep! Somebody should beat him up for not being nice to me. He shouldn't be that way!

_____ Danny's not a very nice person.

_____ Jogging is better for you than swimming.

_____ Jogging increases your pulse rate.

_____ People who don't go jogging are just lazy! Everybody should jog!

17

Facts & Beliefs about Situations

Work in groups to think of 3 Facts and 3 Beliefs about one of the pictures below.

5. Junk-Thought: Food for Misery

As we learned in the last chapter, facts cause very few problems. But the beliefs we have **about** those facts or events can really make us miserable. So, let's take a closer look at beliefs.

Probably the most accurate way to examine our belief system is to study our language. This means both the language we say out loud and also what we keep inside our heads. The language we think, but might not say, is called "self-talk." We don't even realize we're doing it much of the time. It is all the "stuff" that goes on in our heads **about** ourselves, **about** other people, and **about** what happens. It can be very negative and irrational. When it is, it can have the same affect on us as junk food: it can make us miserable. So we'll call this kind of thinking "junk-thought."

Junk-thought

Junk-thought will make us feel absolutely miserable if we let it.

How do we know when we're using junk-thought? What is the language that goes along with it?

There are certain words and phrases that are signals that we are being irrational. For a little help with that, let's meet somebody. I'd like to introduce you to . . .

JIM   JANE

Jim and Jane Junkthot, the Junkthot twins

Jim and Jane might not be so bad off if it weren't for their very small vocabulary. They know only a few words. They have lots of cousins, but their cousins don't know very many words either. All of them are loaded with junk-thought. They'll show us some of the language that goes with different kinds of irrational beliefs. The first kind is . . .

1. DEMANDING

The irrational belief may come out in the form of a demand—the idea that people, or ourselves, or the world, should be a certain way, or different than it is. Here are some examples:

"THINGS SHOULD BE DIFFERENT."

DEMANDING

"I **can't** make a mistake!"
"She **should** wear nicer clothes!"
"If he makes a face at me, I'll **just die!**"
"People **have to** be nice to me!"
"I **must** get a horse!"
"That's not fair!"
"I just **have to** win the contest!"
"Bees **shouldn't** sting!"
"If Molly doesn't call, I'll **just die!**"

Notice the language. Jim Junkthot's favorite demanding phrase is "have to." Jane's favorite when she demands is "can't."

The cousins are here for a visit, too:

When we make demands, we end up making ourselves miserable. Why? Because we generally can't control other people, or the way they are, or the way the world it.

Demands are just beliefs parading around pretending to be facts. But they're just beliefs, and that's all they are. They're not rules, or laws, and they're not written in stone. They're only **our** ideas of how things should be, and sometimes they have very little to do with the way things really are.

If we make the demand that we must not make a mistake, we're going to get upset because sooner or later we will make a mistake of some sort. That's just part of being a human (actually, lots of machines I know make mistakes, too). If we make that kind of demand, we are setting things up for a failure. That applies to all demands. People will wear whatever they want; it will rain regardless of our wishes; it is the nature of a bee that it stings as well as produces honey. Until we change our language and accept the way things are, we'll stay upset and miserable.

Does that mean we shouldn't try to work towards change? Of course not. By all means, it is important to make positive changes when and where we can. But everybody has to decide for themselves what they **can** change and what they **can't** change (no matter how upset they get or how hard they try). Nobody is more miserable than the person who keeps trying to change something that just will not change.

21

2. COPPING-OUT

A second kind of junk-thought is called the Cop-Out. It happens when we refuse to take responsiblity for ourselves.

"IT'S NOT MY FAULT!"

COP-OUT

"I couldn't get my homework done because **they** were watching T.V."

"I'd get better grades if only **my teacher** wasn't so mean."

"**You** make me so mad!"

"**She** ruined my whole day."

"Everything would be fine if it weren't for **him**."

"**He** made me do it."

"It's **not my** fault!"

"If only my **dad** made more money, I'd have more friends."

"I can't find my homework; **somebody** must have stolen it."

Notice the language again. The favorite thought that Jim Junkthot uses when he is copping-out is "not me."

JIM

NOT ME

JANE

SOMEONE ELSE

Jane has her favorite, and here are their cousins, too.

YOU HE SHE IT THEY SOME-BODY

This kind of language will keep us miserable for long periods of time. We've convinced ourselves that it isn't our responsibility and that it's somebody else's fault. So we try to change the **other** person, or we try to change **"it."** If we insist on waiting for other people to change, we'll be waiting for a long time, won't we?

3. OVER-GENERALIZATIONS

Isn't it amazing that we have so many ways to make ourselves feel rotten? There are even more. Over-generalizing happens when we take a little bit of information, make a big deal out of it, and then pretend that it's the whole picture.

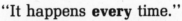

OVER-GENERALIZING

"It happens **every** time."
"I **always** get in trouble."
"He **never** has to help."
"She gets **all** the attention."
"**Nobody** likes me."
"**Everybody** has a 10-speed but me."
"**None** of the other kids have to go to be so early."
"I'm the **only** one who gets such a small allowance."

Does any of the language sound familiar? Here are the Junkthot twins again.

JIM

JANE

And their cousins:

Another way of over-generalizing is to use a word that labels a whole person because of one action they took:

What Happened:
Bud slept until noon.
Over-generalization: "He's **lazy**."

What Happened:
Mom insisted we do our homework.
Over-generalization: "She's **mean**."

Here are just a few labels that indicate over-generalizing. It's all junk-thought and has nothing to do with who the person really is, or what they are really like.

dumb **a jerk** **stupid** **selfish** **dishonest** **a creep**

Like demands and cop-outs, over-generalizations are just beliefs, not facts. They don't make sense and will create problems for the person who uses them.

4. CATASTROPHIZING

This is what we do when we make a mountain out of a mole hill. When something unpleasant or uncomfortable happens, or might happen, we act as if the world is coming to an end. If something happens we don't like, we think it is awful. When somebody is a certain way that we don't like, we think it is just terrible. We act as if we're in the middle of a disaster. Here is the language:

" I'll just DIE IF..."

CATASTROPHIZING

"If anybody sees me with my hair in curls, it will be just **awful!**"

"If I forget a line in the school play, it will be **terrible!**"

"If I have to get up in front of everybody, it will be **horrible!**"

"Isn't it just **awful** the way she wears her hair?"

"Not getting a card on my birthday would be **horrible!**"

"I just **can't stand** the thought of missing the school dance!"

As usual, the language gives it away as junk-thought. Another family reunion of the Junkthots.

Usually irrational beliefs stomp around and are pretty rowdy—especially demands that things should be different. Long after their parents have been divorced, someone is still thinking, "What a rotten deal I got! They shouldn't have done that to me! They should get married again. It's all their fault I'm so unhappy!" As in this case, strong feelings and junk-thought usually go along with irrational beliefs.

But not always. Sometimes irrational beliefs sort of tip toe around and nobody notices them. This is what has happened when we don't seem to have any strong feelings, can't seem to find any junk-thought, and yet we have a pit in our stomach. The irrational belief is hiding, and it lets the person be perfectly calm, relaxed and smiling while they think, "When Mom and Dad get back together, everything will be just fine."

Since everybody has junk-thought, you must have some, too. Start paying closer attention to your "self-talk." Remember, we often aren't even aware that junk-thought is going on. We're so used to this kind of thinking that we hardly pay attention to it. But it definitely is there. Put a little notebook in your pocket and carry it around with you all day for several days. When you start using junk-thought, write it down in the notebook. You'll be amazed at how much of your thinking is junk-thought. Don't necessarily try to change it right now, just **NOTICE IT.** Say to yourself, "Hmm, here I am using junk-thought." And then write it down. We'll work on changing it as we progress.

In summary, we all have irrational beliefs. We all do our share of copping-out, demanding, over-generalizing and catastrophizing. And when we do it, we all experience being upset or miserable.

In the next chapter we'll take a look at some very specific irrational beliefs. Then in the chapters after that we will direct our energy into getting rid of them.

Recognizing Junk-Thought

This is a practice sheet for recognizing different kinds of junk-thought. Can you determine which sentence is an over-generalization, a demand, a cop-out or catastrophizing? Put the initials **"O-G"** or **"D"** or **"C"** or **"C-O"** in front of the sentence.

A. *What Happened:*

Dad frowned when I asked for a new bike for my birthday.

B. *Thoughts & Beliefs about What Happened:*

_____ *"I just **have** to have a new bike."*

_____ "If I don't get one, it will be just **awful**."

_____ "If I have a crummy birthday, it will be all **his** fault."

_____ "He's so **mean.** He **never** gives me neat things."

_____ "**Everybody** gets bikes for their birthday."

_____ "I **can't stand** my old bike; it's **horrid**."

_____ "**All** the kids will laugh at me and make fun."

_____ "Kids don't ask me to go riding 'cause **he** makes me keep my jerky ole bike."

Irrational Language

Here is an event. Work alone or in groups and think of junk-thought that would show the different ways of being irrational.

A. What Happened:

A big party is coming up and you weren't invited.

B. Thoughts & Beliefs about What Happened:

Demand:_____

Demand:_____

Over-generalization:_____

Over-generalization:_____

Cop-out:_____

Cop-out:_____

Catastrophizing:_____

Catastrophizing:_____

Demands Keep us Unhappy

Demands are one of the most common forms of being irrational. We make demands on ourselves, on others, and on the world. What are yours?

DEMANDS I MAKE ON MYSELF:

I have to_____

I have to_____

I can't_____

I can't_____

I should_____

I should_____

I shouldn't_____

I shouldn't_____

DEMANDS I MAKE ON OTHERS:

People should_____

People should_____

People shouldn't_____

People shouldn't_____

Can you extend the list to include demands you make on the world or on life? What cop-outs do you use? What over-generalizing and catastrophizing?

What Can We Change?

Have a class discussion about what we can change and what we can't change. You may wish to explore questions like: Can we make others **feel** a certain way? **think** a certain way? **behave** a certain way?

Can you identify areas in your life where you have tried and tried to change things, but found that those things just will not change? If your parents are separated, can your demands **make** them get back together? If you want someone to be your friend, can you **get** them to like you? After discussing these ideas, make some notes to yourself.

These are some things I will probably not be able to change, no matter how upset I get, and no matter how hard I try. I will work on accepting them:

" I DON'T LIKE IT, BUT I CAN LIVE WITH IT. "

1. _____

2. _____

3. _____

4. _____

These are some things I can change, either in a small way or in a big way. I will work on changing them:

1. _____

2. _____

3. _____

4. _____

6. Beliefs That Cause Problems

Let's pretend for a moment that we are all wearing invisible glasses. And that those glasses come with lots and lots of different lenses. We can change lenses whenever we choose. Take out this set, put in that set. Take out that set, replace it with another set. Decide that set is no longer useful? Throw it out.

The lenses are not regular, ordinary lenses. Instead, they represent beliefs or ideas, and they influence how we see life. They affect what we do, think and feel.

Imagine a three-year old child who walks into a store with his father. He comes around a corner and there, in front of him, is a shelf full of candy. The child has on his invisible glasses. Out goes one set of lenses and in comes a new set. The new lenses (let's give them a number, say, lens set #6) is the belief that says "I MUST HAVE CANDY TO BE HAPPY!" It is the child's belief or idea that "I **need** candy to be happy. If I can't have all the candy I want, right now, I will be **miserable**! It will be **awful**! The world will come to an end! I will just die!"

What happens when the child's father says "No"? Does the world come to an end? Does the child die? Of course not. The child may cry and scream and kick and hit, but, five minutes later, he is laughing and happy. The world has not ended; the child is still breathing; grass is still growing.

The child's belief, "I MUST HAVE CANDY TO BE HAPPY" doesn't make sense; it was nonsense, silly, and not true. Such a belief or idea that does not make sense is an "irrational" idea. We all have irrational ideas. We also have "rational" ideas—ideas that **do** make sense.

At some point in the child's life (after lots of crying, screaming, and kicking) he is going to begin to take lenses out of the box and spread them out. He will begin to study them and to question them. "Do I really want to keep on using this lens? Sometimes it causes me problems". It might have been nice if the child's father could go get lens #6 and throw it out. But, only the child can do that. After some time he will understand that lens set #6 causes him lots of problems and that the idea doesn't make sense. Then he will throw it out.

The rest of this chapter contains eleven of the irrational beliefs or ideas that can cause problems. We may hold to some of these ideas and not to others. These thoughts were identified by Ellis (1962) and are useful. They can help us understand why we feel bad sometimes. They are **ideas about what we think life in this world is or should be**. When we think life **should** be one way and it turns out that it is **not** that way, something has to happen! Either we have to be upset a whole lot of the time, or something has to change. Let's see, what are the options? The world can change or I can change. Can I change the world?

1. EVERYBODY MUST LOVE ME!

The idea that we need love and approval **all the time**. If we don't get enough, we feel awful. We think, "Nobody loves me. I must be awful! I'm such a crumb!" We feel sorry for ourselves ("Poor me!") The most important thing is to "get love". We will do anything for more love.

2. I MUST BE GOOD AT EVERYTHING!

The idea that we must do everthing well to feel good about ourselves. We can't fail. If someone else wins, we feel awful. We say to ourselves, "I lost, so I'm no good. I failed, so I'm lousy. I came in 2nd., how awful!" But the fear of failure can keep us from doing a good job.

3. SOME PEOPLE ARE BAD; THEY MUST BE PUNISHED!

The idea that people who do things that we don't like are bad people. They should be blamed and punished. We think, "He's bad; he should go to jail. She's terrible; we should get rid of her. They are evil; they should go to prison." We can feel that way about ourselves too.

4. THINGS SHOULD BE DIFFERENT!

The idea that it is awful when things are different than the way we want them to be. We think "How terrible; things are just awful." We can't accept things the way they really are. We get upset if we can't change things to fit **our** ideas of what they should be. But there is no reason we should like everything.

5. IT'S YOUR FAULT I FEEL THIS WAY!

The idea that somebody **else** makes us feel the way we do. If we are unhappy, it is because of what someone else said or did. "It's not **my** fault that I'm unhappy," we say. "**You** make me feel mad. **You** make me upset. Other people should change so that I will feel better. It's their job to change. I can't help it."

6. I KNOW SOMETHING BAD WILL HAPPEN—SOON!

The idea that we need to always watch out for things to go wrong. "A car may hit me. A dog may bite me. A lion may eat me on the way to school. I will worry about it so I can be ready for it. I need to keep watching. I can't relax."

7. IT'S EASIER NOT TO EVEN TRY!

The idea that it is easier to avoid difficult tasks in life than to face them. Life is too hard, so we should not try. It is far better to give up. We think, "I give up! I want it to be easy. I can't try. It's too hard. I don't want to take the responsibility."

8. I NEED SOMEONE STRONGER THAN ME!

The idea that we should depend on other people who are stronger than us. The feeling that "I am weak. I can't make my own decisions. Tell me what to think and do. Take care of me." But we are different from everyone else. We will need to learn to make our own decisions because we know ourselves best.

9. I CAN'T HELP BEING THIS WAY.

The idea that things happened to us when we were little, and that made us the way we are. "I'll probably always be this way. The past is the most important thing. There is no hope that I could change."

10. I SHOULD GET UPSET ABOUT YOUR PROBLEMS.

The idea that other people's problems should become our problems. The feeling that we need to change other people. The feeling that it is our job to solve other people's problems and to fix everything in their lives. Their problems are now our problems. We think "I'll take care of you. I'll take your problems."

"ONE WAY IS BEST."

11. THERE IS ONLY ONE GOOD WAY TO DO IT.

The idea that there is one right way to do things and the other ways are no good. Only one way is best. If we don't do something the best way, it will be awful. We think, "He shouldn't do it that way. His way is all wrong. We have to do it exactly this way. If I don't find the perfect way I'll ruin it."

ACTIVITIES

Which Irrational Thoughts are being used?

Below are some Irrational Thoughts. Review the chapter and decide which thought is being used:

_____ "It's too hard. I give up."

_____ "What if I don't get First Place!"

_____ "You decide for me. You take care of it for me."

_____ "If I do good people will love me more."

_____ "People should be different."

_____ "I just know something awful is going to happen!"

_____ "We're going to do it *this way!*"

_____ "It's all *your* fault I got so upset!"

_____ "He's just awful. He should be in jail."

_____ "Don't you worry about it. Leave your problems to

me. I'll take care of everything."

_____ "I've been this way so long; I don't think I can

change."

_____ "I'm no good."

Where do irrational beliefs come from? This is an important question to ask if we really want to get rid of them.

They come from a number of sources: Friends—adults—T.V.—commercials—billboards—magazines—movies.

Advertisers make a lot of money off our misery. They're very smart people. They understand that if they can make us believe that we just **have to** have their product in order to "be happy," then we will buy it. But it doesn't work that way. We end up feeling pretty much the same; they end up with our allowance. **People who can get us to act on our irrational beliefs do indeed have a lot of control over us.** The person who has a belief that he just **has to** smoke to be tough will part with his allowance at the first cigarette machine he sees. The ad-men love it!

Advertising language is full of "shoulds" and "what-ifs" and "have tos." The ads don't say that directly, of course. They hint at it.

Gather some magazines designed for teens and tear out some of the advertisements. Study both the pictures **and** the language. You'll find lots of irrational beliefs hinted at. What kind of junk-thought do the advertisements elicit in people?

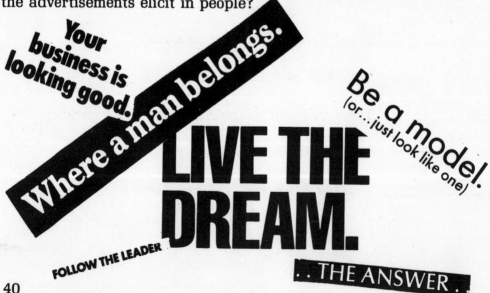

7. "I Hope Your Mouth Falls Off!"

How do we know if we have irrational beliefs? And then, how do we decide **which** ones we have?

We are not concerned here with rational beliefs. They make sense and cause no problems. The real trouble-makers are the irrational beliefs, the ones that don't make sense and are not true. Here are two "keys" for finding irrational beliefs.

The first is:

A. Do you feel **upset**?
B. Do you have **strong** emotions
   such as the ones pictured below?

It is possible to get upset and to have strong emotions for a reason other than an irrational belief. However, getting upset and feeling strong emotions (negative ones) usually means that some irrational beliefs are causing problems. The second "key" is:

A. Do you use judgemental language?
Notice the words you use.

Should!   Ought!   Must!   Awful!   Terrible!

Strong use of these words probably means that you have irrational beliefs.

Once we have noticed strong upset feelings and strong judgemental language we know that some of our thinking is causing us problems and should be changed. The next questions is . . . How do I know **which** irrational beliefs I have?

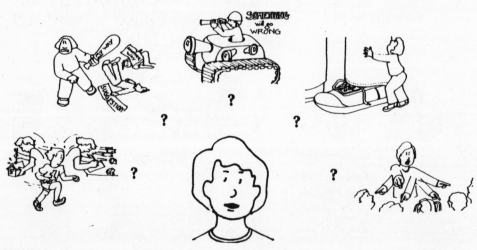

Kranzler suggests 3 easy steps that will help us to then decide which beliefs are causing problems.

STEP ONE:

Describe your feelings. When you feel a strong negative emotion, describe it as well as you can. Use the sentence, "I feel _____." Remember, this is part C, the feeling.

C

STEP TWO:

Describe what happened before the feeling. Describe as well as you can exactly what happened just before the painful feeling started. This is part A. Did someone do something? Say something? Was it something that someone else **might** do? Or might say? Was it something about the way the world is that you don't like? Did **you** do something?

A

STEP THREE:

Describe your thoughts: What did you say to yourself? Be as exact as you can; put down everything you said to yourself in part **B**. This is a difficult step because often we don't know that we are using self-talk. We do it without thinking about it. So, stop and think about what went through your mind.

B

1. SOMETIMES PEOPLE TEASE ME.
2. TED MADE ME SO MAD I FLUNKED MY MATH TEST AND IT'S ALL HIS FAULT!!
3. TED'S JUST AWFUL!
4. TED SHOULD BE DIFFERENT!
5. NOBODY LIKES ME!
6. I HOPE HIS ROTTEN MOUTH FALLS OFF!

Now we are ready to identify which irrational thoughts are causing problems. Study each statement. First ask, "Is that a *Fact* or a *Belief*? If the statement is a *Fact*, it is probably true and shouldn't cause any problems.

Two of the statements this person made are facts—everyone would probably agree that they are true.

> Sometimes people tease me.
> Ted called me "Dumbo Ears."

All of the other statments (we call them "self-talk") are examples of *Beliefs*. We recall that there are some beliefs that make sense and some that don't make sense. We can find signs of irrational thinking in this person's statements. He says things that don't make sense. He uses "awful" and "should." He generalizes —"Nobody likes me," and "People should be different."

44

Review the Eleven Irrational Beliefs in Chapter 5. Then list the statements and put the number next to them that tells which of the Eleven Irrational Beliefs is being used:

__#5__ 2. Ted made me so mad I flunked my math test and it's all HIS FAULT!

__# 3__ 3. Ted's just awful!

__# 4__ 4. Ted should be different!

__# 1__ 5. Nobody likes me!

__general__ 7. I hope his rotten mouth falls off!

We see that this person is using several different Irrational Beliefs. Recognizing them may take some time and practice, but it will get easier.

The person in the example is feeling pretty miserable. Let's put his emotional pain into the **A B C** format:

EMOTIONAL PAIN

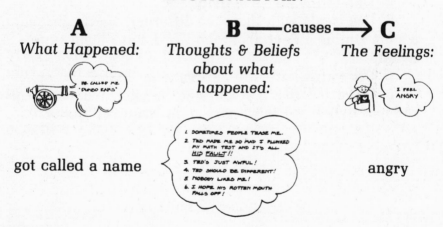

A	**B** ——causes——➤	**C**
What Happened:	*Thoughts & Beliefs about what happened:*	*The Feelings:*
got called a name		angry

Remember that he is feeling miserable and upset not because of what happened, but because of his **thoughts** about what happened.

If he wants to feel better, he needs to change his thinking. Let's look at how that can be done.

45

ACTIVITIES

Facts & Beliefs Circle Activity

Get 5 index cards, 3"x 5". Write one of the following words on each card: school, money, friends, grades, people. Put the cards in a stack face down. Sit with friends, family, or peers in a circle around the cards. The first person takes a card and states a **Fact** about the word on the card. That person then hands the card to any other person in the group, who takes the card and states another **Fact** about the word. That person gives the same card to a third person who states still another **Fact**. Then the card is placed next to the pile and the person to the right of the 1st person to talk picks up a new card and starts over. Do the same for all of the cards.

Variations of the above activity:
    a. Use cards with those (or different) words. Instead of each person stating a **Fact** about the word, have them state a **rational Belief**.
    b. Use cards but state an **irrational Belief**.
    c. Have the first person state a **Fact**; the second person a **rational Belief**; the third person an **irrational Belief**.

8. New Language

To simplify things somewhat, we can look at junk-thought as just a bad habit. Our brain, being like a computer, has adopted certain belief systems (from whatever source) and has been spouting out the same junk-thought over and over. So we'll want to re-program. We'll take out the computer cards with the old beliefs on them, and insert new cards with beliefs that make more sense. The language that comes out will be new language to go along with the new beliefs. And along with the new language, we'll experience a change in our feelings. It won't happen all of a sudden, like it might on a real computer, but after awhile everything will be different. There is a little glinch here. If we go along with using the new language, but still hold onto the old beliefs, we won't get very far. We have to get rid of the beliefs, create fresh, new language, and feelings will change naturally.

The first step in letting go of an old irrational belief is to look at our language when we're feeling upset. What have we been thinking about ourselves, about others, about what happened? You may want to just notice it and make some observations: Hmmm, it seems like my language has a lot of junk-thought in it. Things like: 'I never do anything right. I always mess up. It's his fault I blew it. Nobody else does it wrong but me. I'm no good. I can't stand it when I don't do it right.' Then go behind the language and poke around until you find the belief behind it: "Hmmm, it sounds like I have this idea that *I CAN'T MAKE MISTAKES*. That sounds a lot like the irrational belief that *I MUST DO EVERYTHING WELL*." Now the fun starts. You're onto what its been up to, and now you can confront it:

"AH-HA, YOU RASCAL OF AN OLD BELIEF! I CAUGHT YOU RED-HANDED TRYING TO RUIN MY DAY! YOU ROTTEN RAT! GET OUT AND TAKE YOUR JUNK-THOUGHT WITH YOU. IF YOU COME BACK, I'M GOING TO THROW YOU OUT AGAIN. YOU STAY AWAY FROM ME!"

Good work. Now to replace it with a belief that makes more sense, but even more importantly, one that won't make you upset and miserable. The new belief is this:

IT IS O.K. TO MAKE MISTAKES.

and with the new belief comes new language:

"It is O.K. to make a mistake. Making mistakes is something we all do, and I am still a fine and worthwhile person when I make mistakes. There is no reason for me to get upset when I make a mistake. I am trying, and even if I make a mistake, I am going to continue trying. I can handle making a mistake."

48

It will feel a bit strange at first, because you've had years and years of living with old belief systems and old language and have gotten used to them. But now that we know they're out to make us miserable, it's time to say good-bye to them.

Learning to change our thinking isn't much different than learning baseball, or sewing, or how to draw. It's a skill. Once you get the idea, you just go out and start practicing. And the more you practice, the better you get. The better you get, the easier it is and the more enjoyable it becomes. As it becomes less of a struggle and more of a joy, you will begin to **want** to practice it more, and you will do even better. Pretty soon it has become easy. You look back to when you first began practicing and can't *believe* how hard it was; it seemed impossible, but you kept practicing, and now here your are, good at it!

You deserve mountains of credit for work well done.

We'll look at new language for Demanding, Over-Generalizing, Copping-Out, and Catastrophizing. Then each of the Eleven Beliefs That Cause Problems will be re-defined as new beliefs with new language. This is not a complete list, but will serve as a start.

NEW LANGUAGE OF SHOWING PREFERENCES:

I prefer ...   It's O.K. if ...

I want ...

I would really like it if ... I don't like ...

I'd rather ...   I don't care for ...

NEW LANGUAGE OF TAKING RESPONSIBILITY

I am responsible for ...   Other people aren't responsible for ...

It's my responsibility to . ..Nobody else is responsible for ...

I'm the one who will   Other people don't make me feel ...
      need to ...

It's up to me to ...   It's not up to ...... to ......

I made myself feel ...

NEW LANGUAGE FOR ELIMINATING GENERALIZATIONS:

... a lot ...

Sometimes it seems like ...

... are behaving like ...

... is acting like ...

NEW LANGUAGE FOR ELIMINATING CATASTROPHIZING:

I don't like ...

It will be a little embarrassing, but I'll survive.

I would feel badly if ...

I hope ... (x) ... doesn't happen. But if it does, I'll be O.K.

ELEVEN BELIEFS THAT WILL NOT CAUSE PROBLEMS

EVERYBODY DOESN'T HAVE TO LOVE ME.

1. Not everybody has to love me, or even like me. I don't necessarily like everybody I know, so why should everybody else like me? I enjoy being liked and being loved, but if somebody doesn't like me, I will still be O.K. and still feel like I am an O.K. person. I cannot "make" somebody like me any more than someone can get me to like them. I don't need approval all the time. If someone does not approve of me, I will still be O.K.

IT IS O.K. TO MAKE MISTAKES

2. It is O.K. to make a mistake. Making mistakes is something we all do, and I am still a fine and worthwhile person when I make mistakes. There is no reason for me to get upset when I make a mistake. I am trying, and even if I make a mistake, I am going to continue trying. I can handle making a mistake. It is O.K. for others to make mistakes, too. I will accept mistakes in myself and also mistakes that others make.

OTHER PEOPLE ARE O.K. AND I AM O.K.

3. People who do things I don't like are not necessarily bad people. They should not necessarily be punished just because I don't like what they do or did. There is no reason why another person should be the way I want them to be, and there is no reason why I should be the way somebody else wants me to be. People will be whatever they want to be, and I will be whatever I want to be. I cannot control other people, or change them. They are who they are; we all deserve basic respect and reasonable treatment.

I DON'T HAVE TO CONTROL THINGS

4. I will survive if things are different than what I want them to be. I can accept things the way they are, accept people the way they are, and accept myself the way I am. There is no reason to get upset if I can't change things to fit my idea of how they ought to be. There is no reason why I should have to like everything. Even if I don't like it, I can live with it.

I AM RESPONSIBLE FOR MY DAY

5. I am responsible for how I feel, and for what I do. Nobody can make me feel anything. If I have a rotten day, I am the one who allowed it to be that way. If I have a great day, I am the one who deserves credit for being positive. It is not the responsibility of other people to change so that I can feel better. I am the one who is in charge of my life.

I CAN HANDLE IT WHEN THINGS GO WRONG

6. I don't need to watch out for things to go wrong. Things usually go just fine, and when they don't, I can handle it. I don't have to waste my energy worrying. The sky won't fall in; things will be O.K.

IT IS IMPORTANT TO TRY

7. I can. Even though I may be faced with difficult tasks, it is better to try than to avoid them. Avoiding a task does not give me any opportunities for success or joy, but trying does. I will try even if I don't want to. I would like for it to be easy, but not everything will be easy. Things worth having are worth the effort. I might not be able to do everything, but I can do something.

I AM CAPABLE

8. I don't need someone else to take care of my problems. I am capable. I can take care of myself. I can make decisions for myself . . . I can think for myself. I don't have to depend on somebody else to take care of me.

I CAN CHANGE

9. I can change. I don't have to be a certain way because of what has happened in the past. Every day is a new day. It's silly to think I can't help being the way I am. Of course I can.

OTHER PEOPLE ARE CAPABLE

10. I can't solve other people's problems for them. I don't have to take on other people's problems as if they were my own. I don't need to change other people, or fix up their lives. They are capable and can take care of themselves, and can solve their own problems. I can care and be of some help, but I can't do everything for them.

EVERYONE HAS SOMETHING WORTHWHILE TO CONTRIBUTE

11. There is more than one way to do something. More than one person has good ideas that will work. There is no one and only "best" way. Everybody has ideas that are worthwhile. Some may make more sense to me than others, but everyone's ideas are worthwhile, and everyone has something worthwhile to contribute.

Replacing Irrational Beliefs

Choose an event that could activate old, irrational beliefs. Some could activate more than one. Write down an old, irrational belief that might be there and the language that might go along with it. Then replace it with a new, rational belief and the new language to accompany it. Set up some role playing activities.

A. *What Happened:*

B. *Beliefs about What Happened:*

Old, irrational belief: _____

Language that went with it: _____

_____

_____

New belief: _____

New language: _____

_____

_____

somebody called you "stupid"

didn't get invited to a party

didn't get what you most wanted for your birthday

left homework at home; went back and missed bus

9. Making Changes

Changing our thoughts and feelings can help us avoid hurt. It is very possible to change our beliefs and ideas, but it requires time and practice. It won't happen if our minds are racing through the day, too busy to stop and be aware of what we are thinking. We need to slow down and carefully examine our beliefs and self-talk.

Basically what we do is **find our irrational thoughts and then change them to rational thoughts that make sense.** Then they will no longer cause so many problems.

Irrational thought: (#4)   **"It's all Ted's fault! He made me so mad I flunked my Math test."**

Counter with rational thought: **I took the test, not Ted.**

Here are some examples of irrational thoughts and some rational thoughts to replace them:

Irrational Thought	Rational Thought
"Some big brother Jim is! The kids tease me and Jim doesn't even **protect** me!" (#8)	"Jim is not on earth to protect me. He won't always be around. Besides, I'm **glad** Jim doesn't protect me. It's his way of showing me that he thinks I can take care of myself. I know if I ever really **needed** Jim he'd help."

"I **must** get an 'A' on my quiz today. If I don't I will **just die!**" (#2)

"It would be nice to get an 'A', and I might feel disappointed if I don't get it, but I'll be O.K. either way. No one has ever died from getting a 'B' on a test, or from getting an 'F.'"

Again we will follow the steps similar to those outlined by Kranzler:

STEP ONE: **Describe the feeling, C;**

STEP TWO: **Describe what happened, A;**

STEP THREE: **Describe thoughts and self-talk, B;**

STEP FOUR: **Identify Irrational Beliefs;**

STEP FIVE: **List Rational Beliefs and rational self-talk.**

Let's give it a try.

STEP ONE:

STEP TWO:

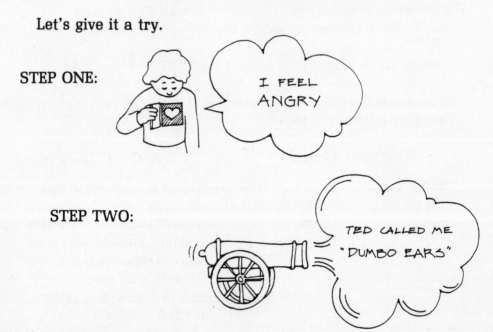

STEP THREE:

STEP FOUR:

Identification of Irrational Beliefs:

Sentence
2. *(#5)* It's your fault!
3. *(#3)* You're awful!
4. *(#4)* Things should be different!
5. *(#1)* Everybody must love me!
7. This is general irrational thinking.

STEP FIVE:

List Rational Beliefs and rational self-talk:

Sentence
2. I took the test, not Ted.
3. Not everyone thinks Ted is awful; his best friend thinks he is great!
4. People are whatever they are. Not everyone will be the way I think would be nice, and I can't be the way everyone else wants me to be, either. Why should he be the way I want? I don't have to like it, but it's not my job to change him.
5. Maybe Ted doesn't like me. Not everybody likes me, and there may be some people I don't like, either. I will do just fine.
7. Just understand that it won't happen.

57

The change in feelings will come from changes we make in our thinking. When our thoughts are more positive, so will be our emotions. Let's look at the new thoughts and new feelings in the **A, B, C** format:

A   B ——causes——→ C

What Happened:	*Thoughts & Beliefs about what happened:*	*The Feelings:*
Got called a name,	1. I am responsible for my grades. 2. Everyone has some good qualities. 3. Why should every-body like me?	O.K., hopeful

The new feeling of "O.K." comes directly from thoughts that have no judgements, no accusations, thoughts that accept things the way they are. Changing our thoughts can be a real effort. We have **habits** in our thinking that we may not even be aware of. And those habits can be negative thoughts that continue to give us negative feelings. So, it is important to learn what our thoughts are so we can understand how they lead us into negative feelings. That takes lots of practice, but the results are worth it. We can begin to feel better both about ourselves and about other people. **Changing is exciting. We may not be able to do much to change the whole world, but we can do a lot to change our little corner of the world.**

ACTIVITIES

Which Irrational Belief has been replaced with New Language?

Below are some Rational Thoughts that will make people feel O.K. Review Chapter 6 and decide which Irrational Thought has been changed by the new statement.

_____ "That's something I can't change, but I can accept it the way it is."

_____ "Everything will be just fine. I will relax and enjoy it."

_____ "I have lots of people who love and care for me. I am loved and valued."

_____ "I don't understand some people and I don't like what some people do, but they are responsible for themselves.

_____ "I am responsible for my own feelings."

_____ "I will not give up."

_____ "I will help if I can, but I cannot solve your problem."

_____ "I can take care of things for myself. I am strong."

_____ "That is an interesting idea. Maybe there are several good answers."

_____ "I am good at some things and not so good at others. That is O.K."

_____ "I am changing all the time. I can choose to change in whatever way I want."

PRACTICE SHEET FOR CHANGING

1. Describe feelings: **(C)**

2. Describe
   what happened: **(A)**

3. Describe self-talk: **(B)**

   Indicate "F" or "B" (Fact or Belief).

F/B

a. _____ ___

b. _____ ___

c. _____ ___

d. _____ ___

e. _____ ___

4. Identify Beliefs that cause problems:

Indicate "D" (Demand), "O-G" (Over-generalization), "C-O" (Cop-out), or "C" (Catastrophizing).

_____ #_____: _____

_____ #_____: _____

_____ #_____: _____

_____ #_____: _____

_____ #_____: _____

5. List new Beliefs that make sense:

#_____: _____

#_____: _____

#_____: _____

#_____: _____

#_____: _____

PRACTICE SHEET FOR CHANGING

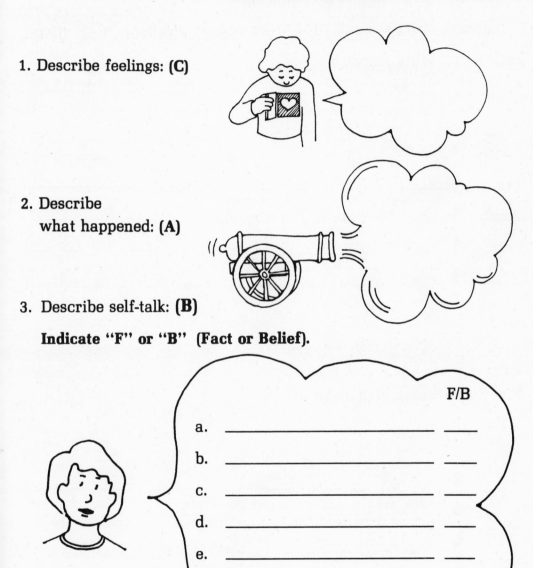

1. Describe feelings: **(C)**

2. Describe
   what happened: **(A)**

3. Describe self-talk: **(B)**

   Indicate "F" or "B" (Fact or Belief).

		F/B
a.		
b.		
c.		
d.		
e.		

4. Identify Beliefs that cause problems:

Indicate "D" (Demand), "O-G" (Over-generalization), "C-O" (Cop-out), or "C" (Catastrophizing).

_____ #_____: _____

_____ #_____: _____

_____ #_____: _____

_____ #_____: _____

_____ #_____: _____

5. *List new Beliefs that make sense:*

#_____: _____

#_____: _____

#_____: _____

#_____: _____

#_____: _____

BIBLIOGRAPHY

Ellis, Albert, REASON AND EMOTION IN PSYCHOTHERAPY.
    1962, Lyle Stuart, New York.

Kranzler, Gerald D., EMOTIONAL EDUCATIONAL EXERCISES FOR
    CHILDREN. 1974, Cascade Press, Eugene, Oregon.

Kranzler, Gerald D., YOU CAN CHANGE HOW YOU FEEL. 1974,
    R.E.T.C. Press, Eugene, Oregon.

Notes

ORDER FORM

Please send me _____ copies of THINKING, CHANGING, REARRANGING. Enclosed is my ☐ check or ☐ money order payable to **Timberline Press** in the amount of:

_____ copies @ $5.95 = $ _____

shipping cost of $1.00 (plus .50 each additional copy) = $ _____

TOTAL = $ _____

Please mail this order with your check to:

TIMBERLINE PRESS
P.O. Box 4348
Estes Park, CO 80517

Thank you for your order. Sorry we cannot ship on credit.

Name _____

Address _____

City, State _____

Zip Code _____

How did you learn about THINKING, CHANGING, REARRANGING?
☐ co-worker ☐ workshops ☐ flyer ☐ other _____

☐ Please send me information regarding workshops in my area.

ORDER FORM

Please send me _____ copies of THINKING, CHANGING, REARRANGING. Enclosed is my ☐ check or ☐ money order payable to **Timberline Press** in the amount of:

_____ copies @ $5.95 = $ _____

shipping cost of $1.00 (plus .50 each additional copy) = $ _____

TOTAL = $ _____

Please mail this order with your check to:

TIMBERLINE PRESS
P.O. Box 4348
Estes Park, CO 80517

Thank you for your order. Sorry we cannot ship on credit.

Name _____

Address _____

City, State _____

Zip Code _____

How did you learn about THINKING, CHANGING, REARRANGING?
☐ co-worker ☐ workshops ☐ flyer ☐ other _____

☐ Please send me information regarding workshops in my area.